HAL LEONARD

GUITAR METHOD

BLUES GUITAR FOR KIDS

A Beginner's Guide with Step-by-Step Instruction for Acoustic and Electric Guitar

BY DAVE RUBIN

WHAT IS THE BLUES?

The blues is the first original American music, made 150 years ago in the South by African-Americans. A lot of modern popular music comes from the blues and now people all over the world love to hear it and play it. It usually contains words and can be played on different instruments like the piano, harmonica, and saxophone. But the guitar is the one you hear the most in the blues.

PLAYBACK+
Speed • Pitch • Balance • Loop

To access audio and online content visit:
www.halleonard.com/mylibrary

Enter Code
2499-1986-3579-5741

ISBN: 978-1-5400-0403-1

Copyright © 2018 by HAL LEONARD LLC
International Copyright Secured All Rights Reserved

No part of this publication may be reproduced in any form or by
any means without the prior written permission of the Publisher.

Visit Hal Leonard Online at
www.halleonard.com

Contact Us:
Hal Leonard
7777 West Bluemound Road
Milwaukee, WI 53213
Email: info@halleonard.com

In Europe contact:
Hal Leonard Europe Limited
42 Wigmore Street
Marylebone, London, W1U 2RN
Email: info@halleonardeurope.com

In Australia contact:
Hal Leonard Australia Pty. Ltd.
4 Lentara Court
Cheltenham, Victoria, 3192 Australia
Email: info@halleonard.com.au

IF YOU ARE NEW TO THE GUITAR

Guitars come in three different sizes:

Guitars also come in three basic types:

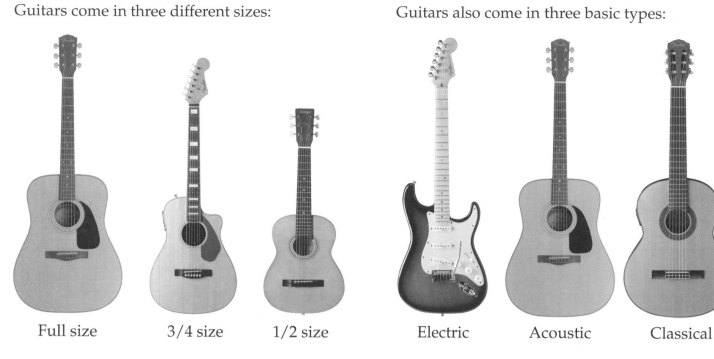

Full size   3/4 size   1/2 size   Electric   Acoustic   Classical

Electric guitars are thinner and usually easier for beginners to hold. Acoustic guitars have a clean, bright sound and are portable. Classical guitars have nylon strings which are often easier on the fingers. Choose a guitar that best fits you.

Too Big   Good Fit

PARTS OF THE GUITAR

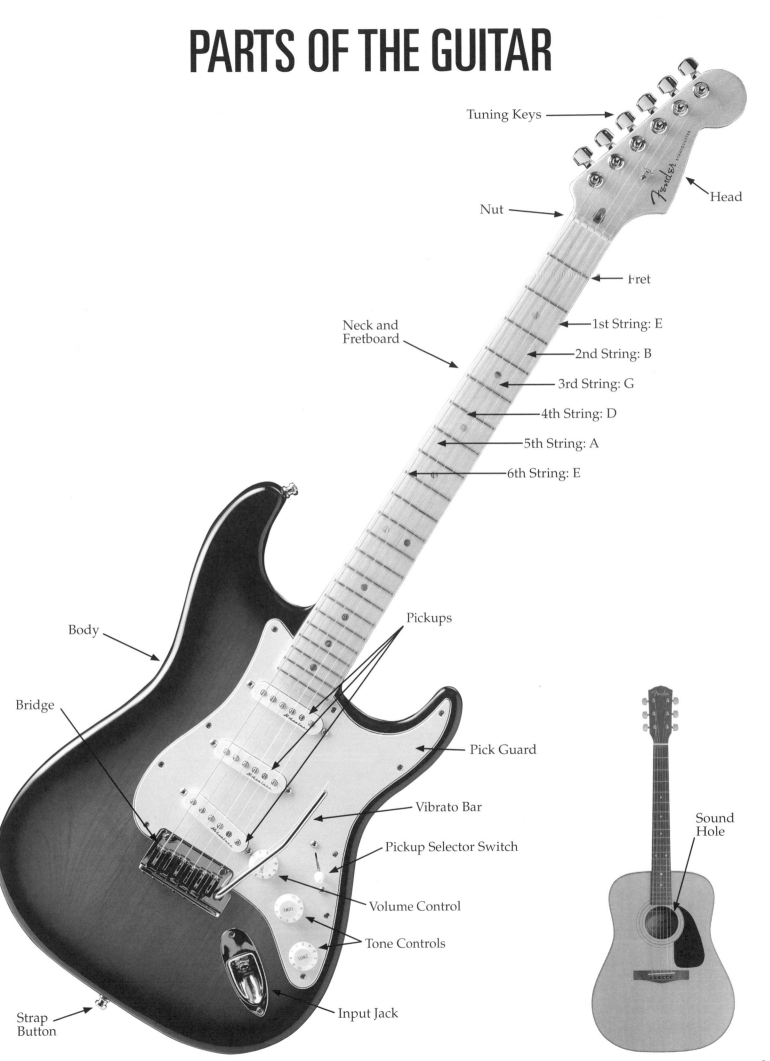

Tuning Keys

Head

Nut

Fret

Neck and Fretboard

1st String: E

2nd String: B

3rd String: G

4th String: D

5th String: A

6th String: E

Body

Pickups

Bridge

Pick Guard

Vibrato Bar

Pickup Selector Switch

Volume Control

Tone Controls

Strap Button

Input Jack

Sound Hole

HOLDING THE GUITAR

- Sit up straight and relax

- Place your feet flat on the floor or place one foot on a foot stool

- Tilt the neck of the guitar slightly upwards

- Raise your thigh to prevent the guitar from slipping; adjust chair or foot stool

- Look at the photos below and match the body position

HAND POSITION

Left Hand

Fingers are numbered 1 through 4.
Press the string firmly between the frets.

Place your thumb in the middle of the back of the neck. Arch your fingers and keep your palm clear of the neck.

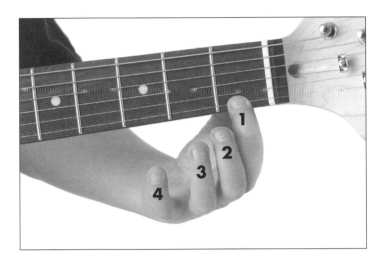

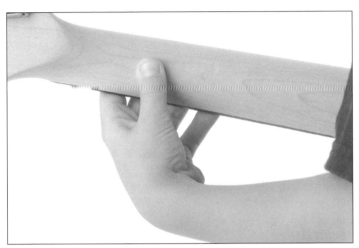

Right Hand

Hold the pick between your thumb and index finger.

Pluck the string with a downward motion of the pick or thumb halfway between the bridge and neck.

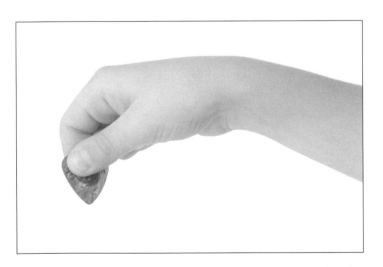

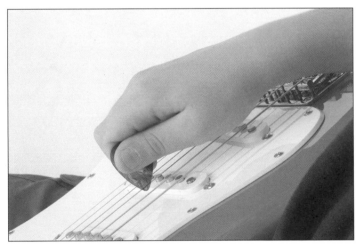

ONLINE AUDIO & MORE

This book comes with online audio tracks, for download or streaming, plus a bonus online tuner and metronome! Ask a parent or teacher to use the code on page 1 to unlock all of the audio tracks, tuner, and metronome at *www.halleonard.com/mylibrary*.

Follow the online directions for the tuner to tune your guitar's strings, and be sure to check out the metronome—a great practice tool that provides a steady beat and improves your rhythm skills!

BLUES GUITAR IS FUN!

Playing blues guitar is the best because you can make up your own music after you learn the main parts of a blues song. We will start with the foundation, which you could see as the bottom section of a house or other building. In the blues, the foundation is the notes or chords over which the vocalist sings or the guitarist solos.

PLAYING BLUES ON THE BASS STRINGS

The bass strings are the three lowest and fattest strings. Let's start building our "blues house" with note patterns on the bass strings using a song form called **12-bar blues**. We will call them "Bass String Riffs."

They are presented in **tablature**, a quick and easy way to see where the notes are on the fretboard while listening to the audio for the rhythm. In tablature (or **tab**), the six lines represent the six guitar strings, starting with the lowest string as the bottom line. The numbers on the lines tell you the frets where your left-hand fingers should push down. A zero (0) means to play that string **open**, without fretting.

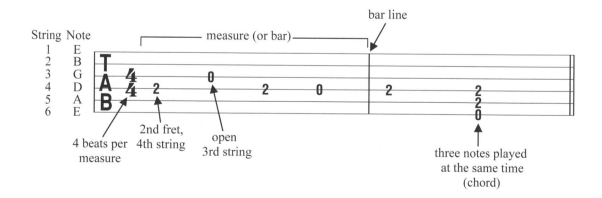

BASS STRING RIFF #1 — KEY OF E 🔊

E is one of the most popular keys for blues guitarists. This riff is similar to "Help Me" by Sonny Boy Williamson and "Green Onions" by Booker T & the MGs. Pick each note with a **downstroke** (using a downward motion, toward the floor) and remember to listen to the demo audio track to hear the rhythm.

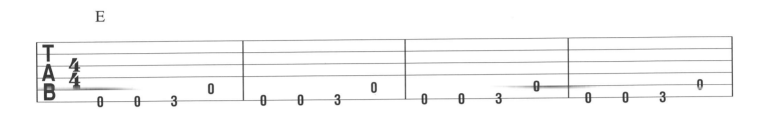

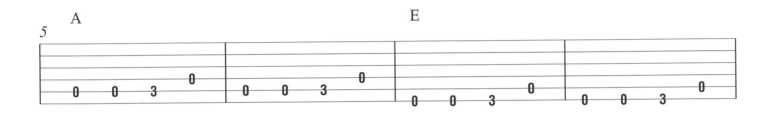

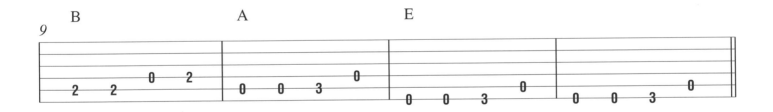

USING THE AUDIO

After you've listened to the audio demo track to hear how it's played, try playing your guitar along with the play-along track. You will hear four clicks, or beats, at the **tempo** (speed) of the song before the music starts. You can do this with all the examples in the book!

BASS STRING RIFF #2 — KEY OF E 🔊

Classic blues songs using a similar riff are "Linda Lu" by Ray Sharpe and "Let Me Love You, Baby" by Buddy Guy. In the ninth **measure** (or **bar**), you'll see fret-hand finger numbers underneath the tab. Practice this measure slowly at first, over and over, until you can play it smoothly.

BASS STRING RIFF #3 — KEY OF E 🔊

Ray Charles used a similar blues riff for his piano hit "What'd I Say." Like the last riff, practice bar 9 slowly.

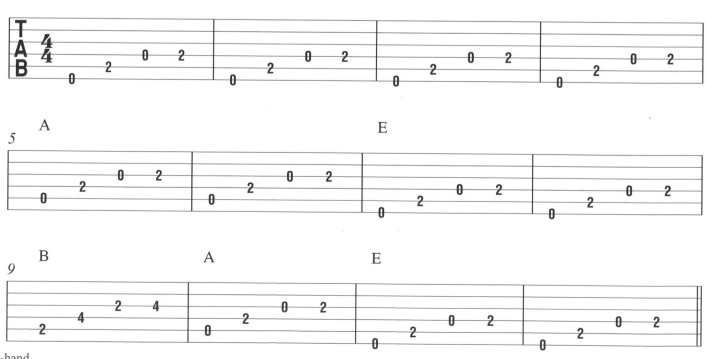

BASS STRING RIFF #4 — KEY OF E 🔊

Riff #4, like #1, has a dark sound due to the second note in each measure.

CHANGING NOTES

As you are playing one note, look ahead to the next and get your fingers ready.

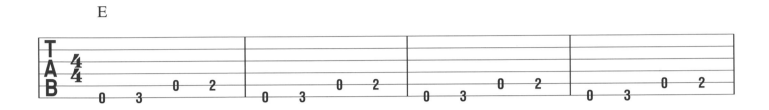

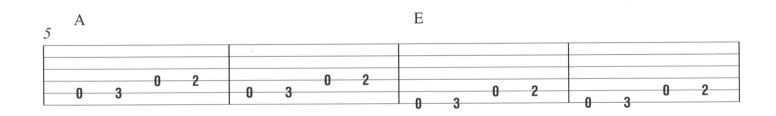

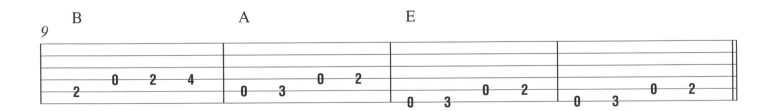

BASS STRING RIFF #5 — KEY OF E

Use fingers 1 and 4 (your index and pinky fingers) to play the fretted notes in this riff, except in bar 9, where it starts with finger 2 (middle finger). Here, you'll need to do a big stretch to reach the notes.

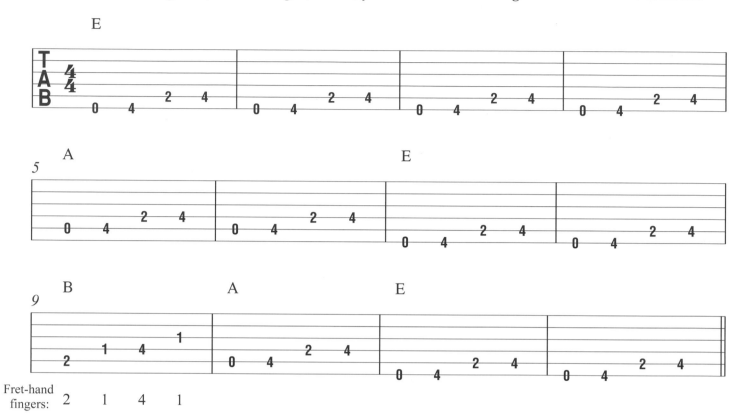

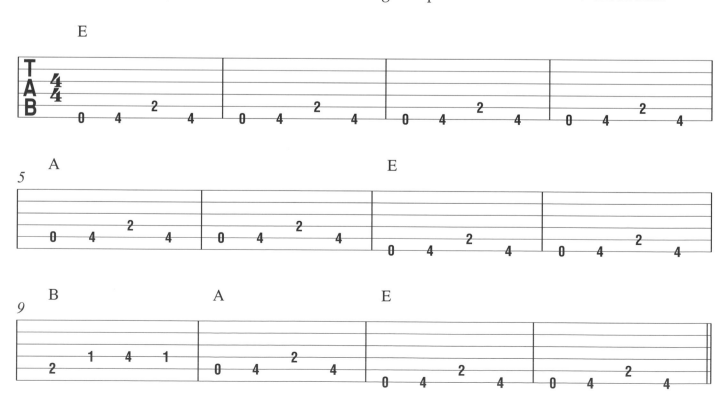

Fret-hand fingers: 2   1   4   1

BASS STRING RIFF #6 — KEY OF E

This riff is similar to #5, but the direction of the notes goes up and down for a different sound.

BASS STRING RIFF #7 — KEY OF A

The key of A is also very popular with blues guitarists. One big reason is because the first notes of each **chord**—A, D, and E—are played with open strings 5, 4, and 6. You'll learn more about chords in the next section.

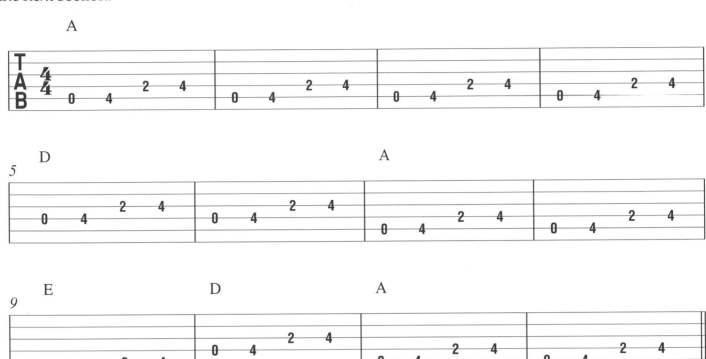

BASS STRING RIFF #8 — KEY OF A

The blues has many different sounds. When the notes of a riff **descend**, or drop down lower in pitch, it can make a spooky sound.

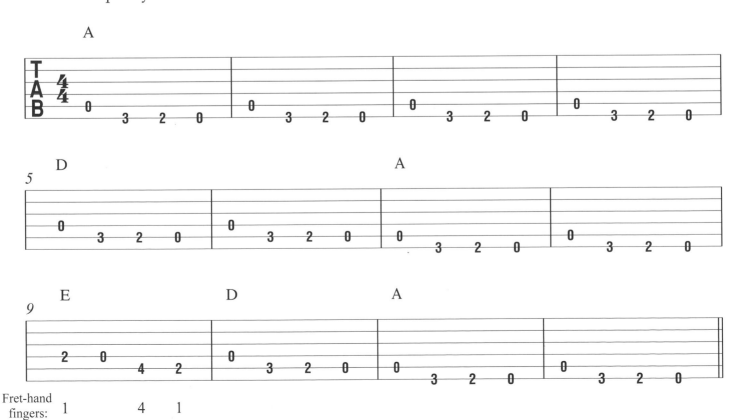

Fret-hand
fingers: 1   4   1

BASS STRING RIFF #9 – KEY OF A

Many famous blues songs use riffs similar to this one, including "Hoochie Coochie Man" by Muddy Waters and "I'm a Man" by Bo Diddley.

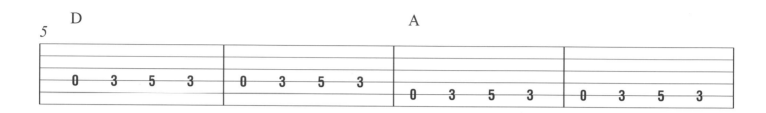

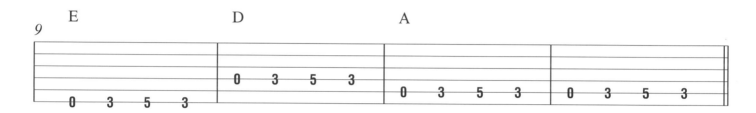

BASS STRING RIFF #10 – KEY OF A

Another type of music related to the blues is boogie woogie. It is often played on the piano as well as the guitar. Riff #10 is similar to boogie woogie music. You can use left-hand fingers 2, 3, and 1 (in that order) to play all the fretted notes in this riff.

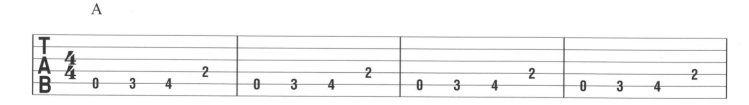

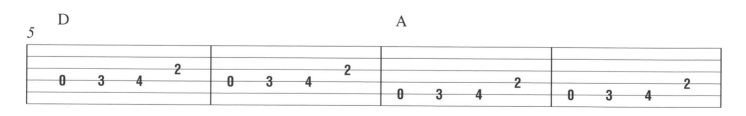

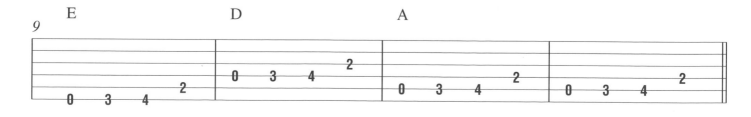

BASS STRING RIFF #11 – KEY OF A

This riff sounds a little like rock 'n' roll. A lot of rock 'n' roll comes from the blues, making it strong and exciting. Notice how the notes for bar 9 "walk" down the low E string for a different idea than the notes for the rest of the riff.

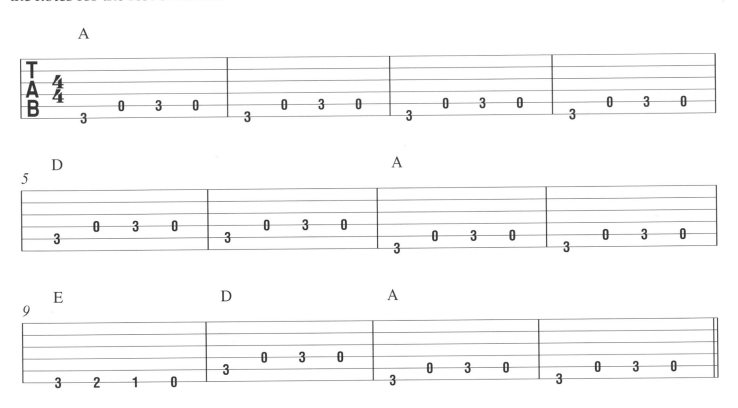

BASS STRING RIFF #12 – KEY OF A

Riff #12 **ascends** (goes up) the scale to make a "happy" blues sound. Any of the 12 Bass String Riffs in this book could be played slow or fast, but this one is best when played faster. If you cannot do it yet, practice slowly until you can!

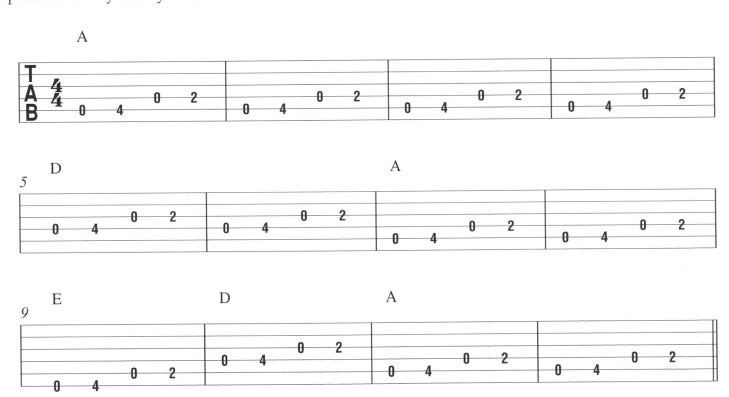

13

PLAYING BLUES WITH CHORDS

There are almost countless ways to play the blues with just three chords. A **chord** is three or more notes played at the same time, but blues and rock guitarists often use two-note chords as well. Let's look at some of the basic ones that all blues guitarists have played.

The chords in this section will be presented in tablature and sometimes with **chord diagrams**. These are grids that show you how to play each chord, with six vertical lines representing the six guitar strings. The lowest string is on the left side, and the highest string is on the right side. The circled numbers show you where to fret with your left-hand fingers, and the open circles and X's tell you which strings to strum.

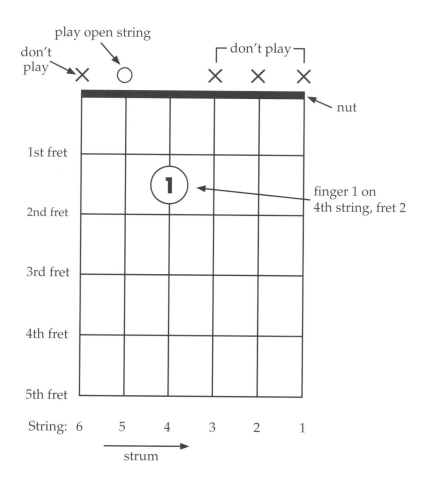

BLUES CHORDS #1 — KEY OF A 🔊

As you play through the next examples, you might notice that the chords change more often than they did in the previous examples. This is another version of the 12-bar blues song form.

12-BAR BLUES

In a 12-bar blues, like you've been playing in this book, musicians will **repeat** the 12-bar cycle over and over to make a full song. You should also do this as you play through the examples. When you get to bar 12, simply repeat back to bar 1 without stopping, and keep playing through the song form as many times as you'd like. Try making up your own words and singing along too!

Strum down on the open string and the fretted note at the same time, being careful to not strike any other strings. Use finger 1 to fret all the notes on the 2nd fret.

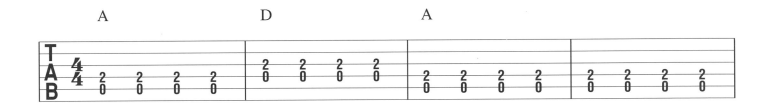

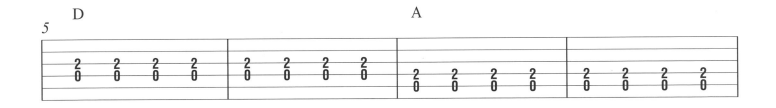

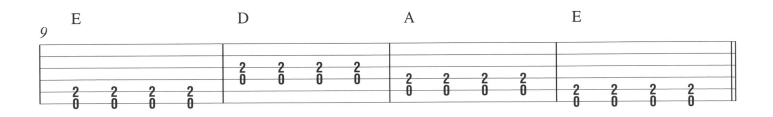

BLUES CHORDS #2 — KEY OF E 🔊

For the B chords, check out the chord diagram below. If fret 4 is too much of a stretch for your third finger, try using finger 4 instead. Strum down on both strings together.

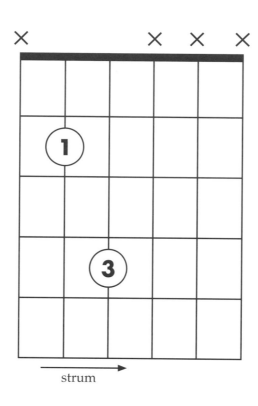

strum

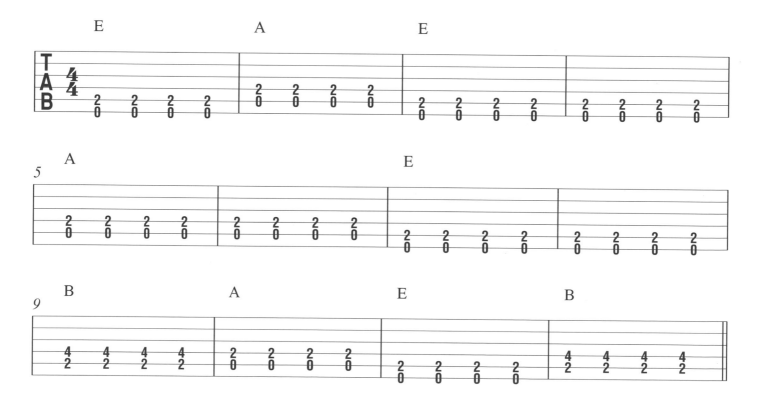

BLUES CHORDS #3 — KEY OF G 🔊

Sometimes playing blues chords can be as easy as starting with a pair of open strings. Strum down on the open strings and then use your first finger to **barre** the pairs of notes for the other chords. This means to fret the two notes with one finger; lay your first finger flat across strings 3 and 4 and push both down with the side of your fingertip.

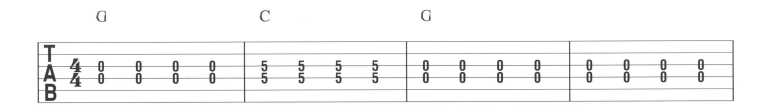

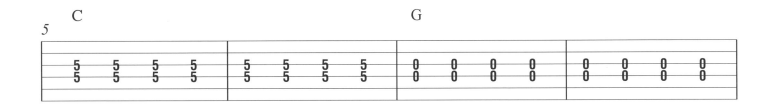

BLUES CHORDS #4 — KEY OF G

This 12-bar blues takes you a step closer to using actual chords. For the G chord, check out the diagram. Use your first finger to barre the C and D chords.

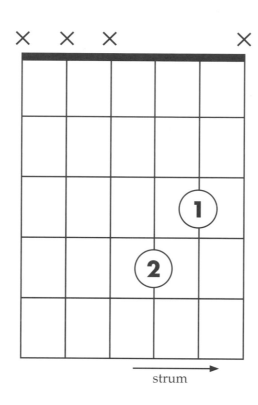

strum

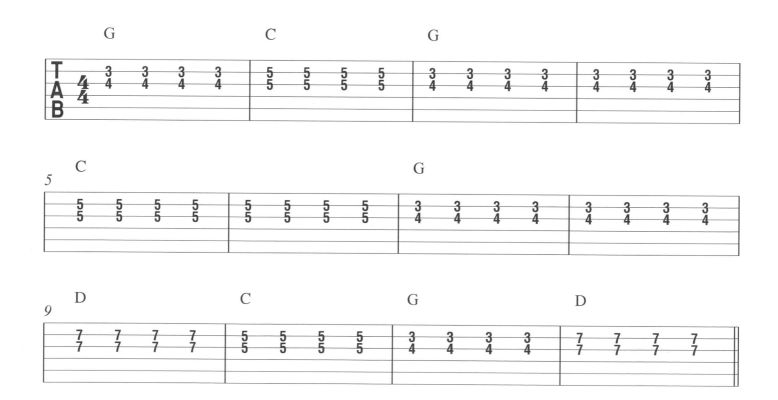

BLUES CHORDS #5 — KEY OF D 🔊

This example uses the highest two strings. For all three chords, place your second finger on string 2 and your first finger on string 1. When you move between chords, just slide this same chord fingering up and down the neck, and make sure you get to each chord on time.

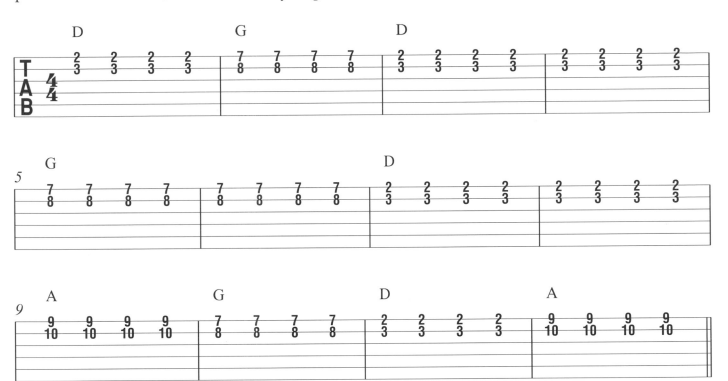

BLUES CHORDS #6 — KEY OF G 🔊

For all three chords in this example, place your third finger on string 4 and your second finger on string 3.

BLUES CHORDS #7 — KEY OF G 🔊

Here are more two-note chords, but now on the lower strings. Place your third finger on string 5 and your second finger on string 4.

BLUES CHORDS #8 — KEY OF G

This last musical example with two-note chords combines them on strings 6 and 5 and on strings 5 and 4.

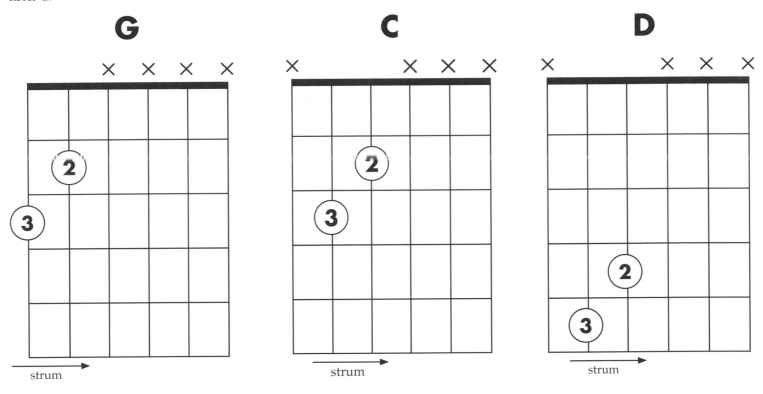

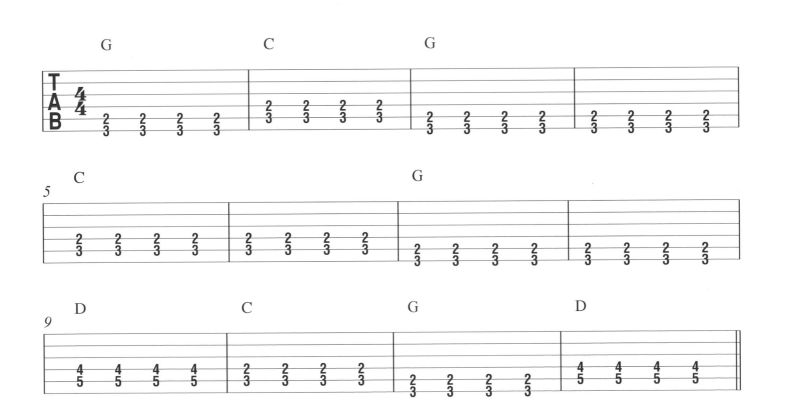

BLUES CHORDS #9 – KEY OF D 🔊

Building on Blues Chords #5, we now have full three-string chords. The types of chords in this example are called **major chords** and have a "happy" sound.

CHANGING CHORDS

As you are playing one chord, look ahead to the next and get your fingers ready. Always keep a steady beat!

Use this fingering for all three chords:

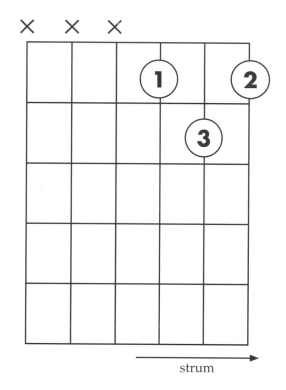

strum

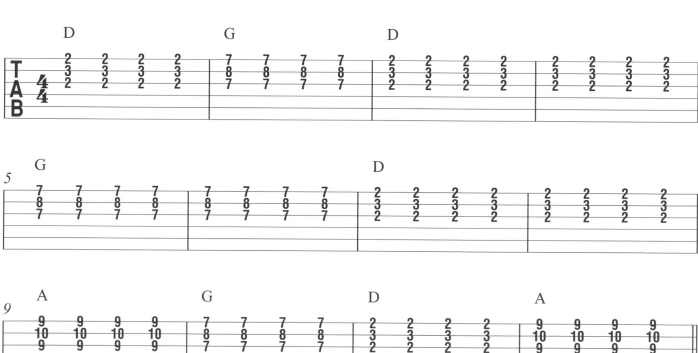

BLUES CHORDS #10 — KEY OF D

Taking an even bigger step forward in learning blues chords, this example contains what are called **seventh chords**, a very common blues sound that you might recognize. Here is the fingering to use on all three chords:

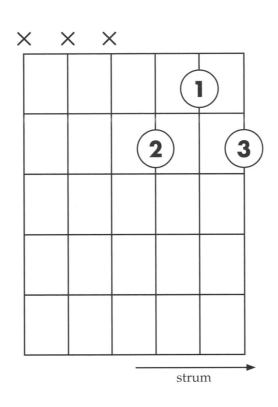

strum

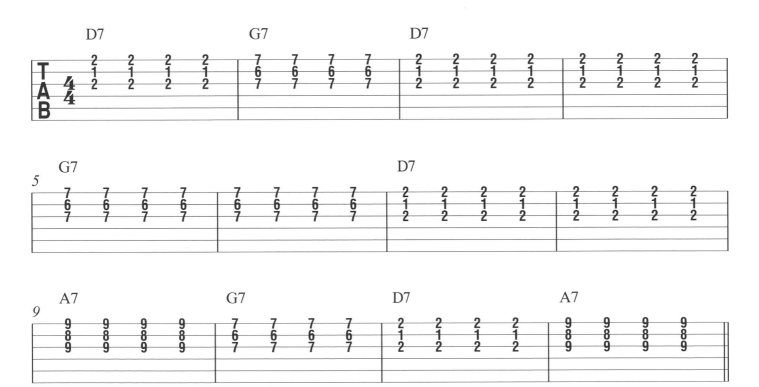

BLUES CHORDS #11 – KEY OF G 🔊

If you take the major chord fingerings used in Blues Chords #9 and move them to another set of
strings, you create seventh chords. Use this fingering on all three chords:

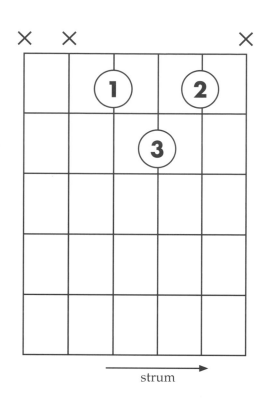

strum

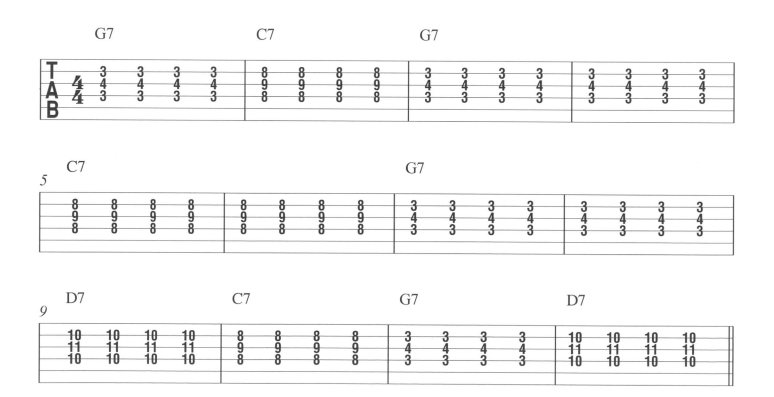

BLUES CHORDS #12 – KEY OF D

This last chord example adds a new D7 chord along with the same fingerings from #11 for the G7 and A7 chords. Here is the fingering for D7:

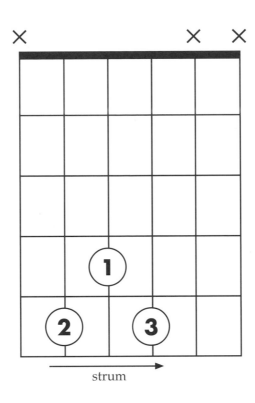

strum

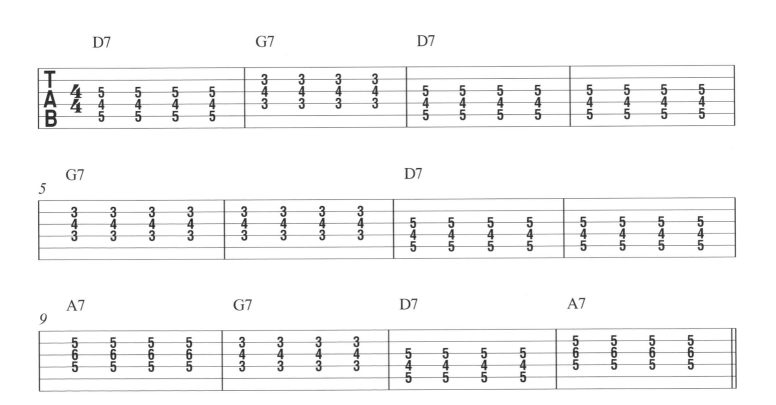

YOU CAN SOLO WITH JUST THREE NOTES

Now the real fun begins! A blues **solo** is usually played in between the vocal verses of a song. It gives guitarists a chance to express themselves in the spotlight. After you learn the following solo ideas, be sure to play with the included play-along tracks so you can try them out with the full band!

After Solo #1, which only uses three different notes, you will see how more can be played as well. Listening to blues songs with guitar solos is the best way to hear how guitarists play with many more notes for an energetic performance!

SOLO #1 – KEY OF A

As an introduction to blues soloing, just play the **root note**, or name of each chord. Pick each note four times in every bar.

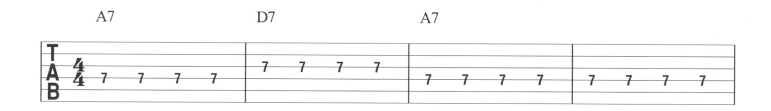

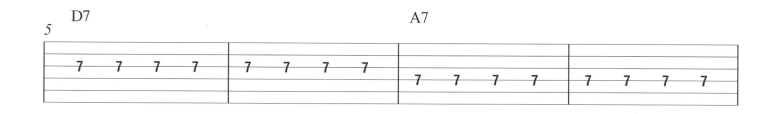

SOLO #2 – KEY OF A

Adding more notes from the chords, along with the root notes, begins to make the solo more interesting. Listen to how the notes in bars 1, 5, and 8 bring out the sound of the chords. As you play each bar, remember to look ahead to the next notes so you can prepare for them.

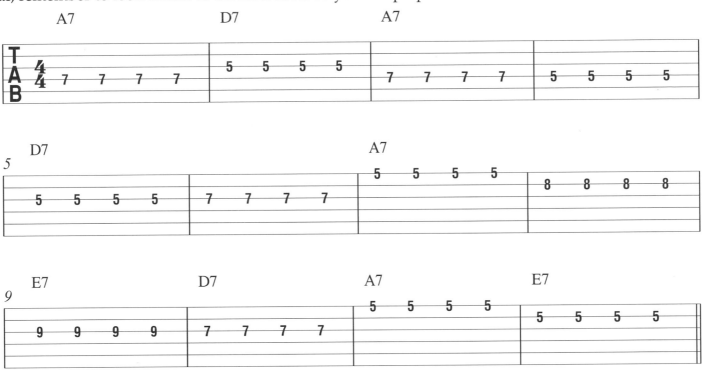

SOLO #3 – KEY OF A

With two different notes in each bar instead of only one, this solo continues to build our "blues house." Use your first finger for the notes on the 5th fret, third finger for the 7th fret, and fourth finger for the 8th fret.

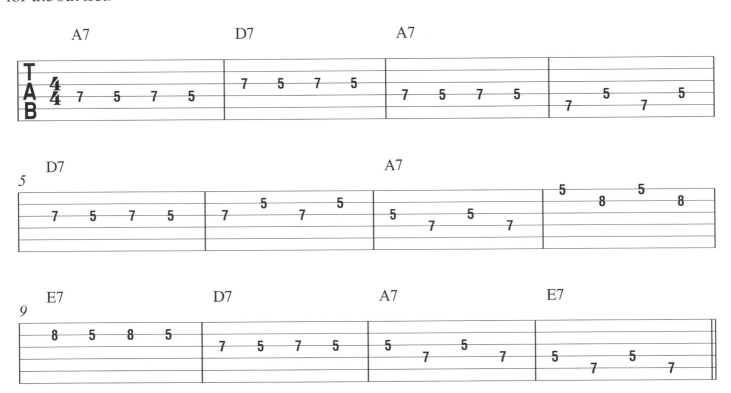

SOLO #4 – KEY OF G 🔊

Notice how bars 1 and 4 have open strings. Certain keys, like G, can be played using open strings. Use fingers 1, 3, and 4 for the fretted notes. Remember to take it slowly at first.

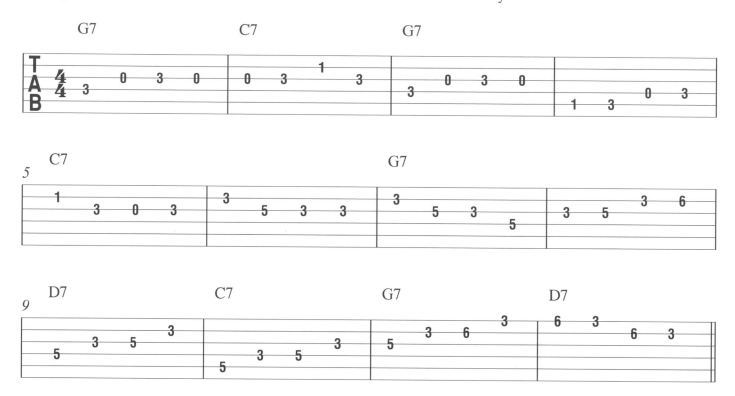

SOLO #5 – KEY OF G 🔊

Sometimes blues guitarists run up and down the scale and other times they go back and forth between a few notes. Bars 9 and 10 are good examples. It makes for variety—an important thing to have in a strong blues solo.

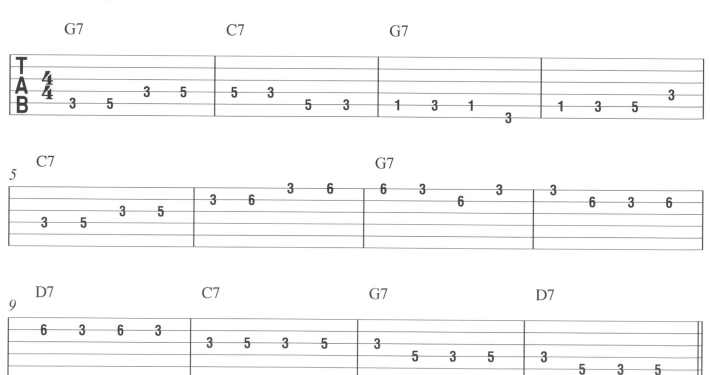

SOLO #6 — KEY OF E 🔊

The key of E is special because all six strings can be played as open notes. Notice bars 10 and 11, in which two notes repeat for variety. Finger 2 should be used for the notes at fret 2 and finger 3 for the notes at fret 3.

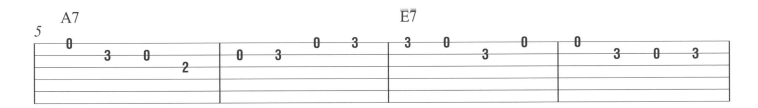

SOLO #7 — KEY OF E 🔊

This solo contains some of the same notes as Solo #6, but they are 12 frets higher on the fretboard. This is called playing up an **octave**—the same notes but in a higher register or range. In bar 11, use your index finger to barre the notes across strings 1, 2, and 3.

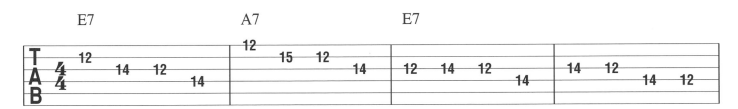

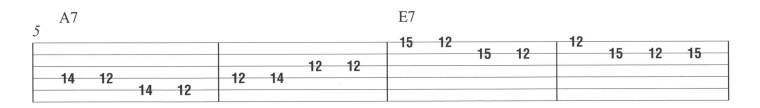

SOLO #8 – KEY OF E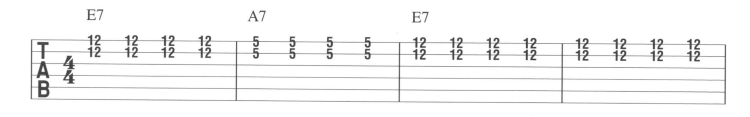

Playing two-note chords is another blues solo idea. This one has the notes following along with the chords for E, A, and B. Use your index finger to barre the notes and be sure to pick them with a fast downstroke.

```
       E7                         A7                      E7
T   4  12    12    12    12    5    5    5    5    12    12    12    12    12    12    12    12
A   4  12    12    12    12    5    5    5    5    12    12    12    12    12    12    12    12
B
```

```
   A7                                        E7
5  5    5    5    5    5    5    5    5    12    12    12    12    12    12    12    12
   5    5    5    5    5    5    5    5    12    12    12    12    12    12    12    12
```

```
   B7                      A7                      E7                      B7
9  7    7    7    7    5    5    5    5    12    12    12    12    7    7    7    7
   7    7    7    7    5    5    5    5    12    12    12    12    7    7    7    7
```

SOLO #9 – KEY OF E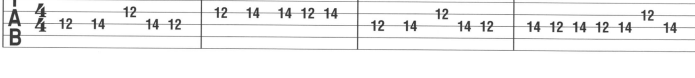

In this solo, some new rhythms are used that add more notes to each measure. Listen to the audio demo to hear how they sound.

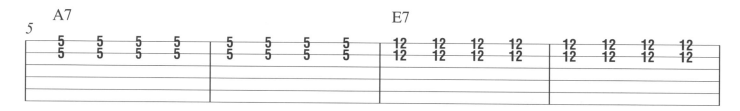

```
       E7                              A7                      E7
T   4              12                 12  14  14  12  14                 12
A   4  12  14         14  12                                    12  14        14  12   14  12  14  12  14      12  14
B
```

```
   A7                                      E7
5  12  14  14  12  14      14  14  12  14  12  14       12  14  14      12      14  12      14  12  14
                                                                14  12
```

```
   B7                      A7                      E7                      B7
9                          12  14  14  12             12  14      12                      12
   12  14  14     12      14               14      12  14     14  12      14  12  14      12  14
               12                                                         14
```

SOLO #10 – KEY OF A

The last few solos include two new blues ideas for you to try. The first is **bending**, which is pushing (or bending) a string to raise the pitch of a note. It is one of the most important parts of blues guitar soloing. In the tab, the notes with the arrows above them are the ones to bend.

The second new idea is a called a **turnaround**, in bars 11 and 12. This is also a very important part of the blues that ends a 12-bar verse while pointing you back (or turning you around) to the beginning of a new verse.

Use your third finger for each bend. The arrow pointing up with "¼" means to push it just far enough to hear the pitch, or sound, go up a small amount. You can pull the string toward the floor or up toward the ceiling.

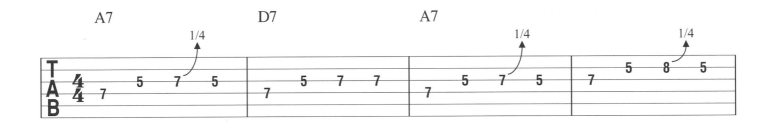

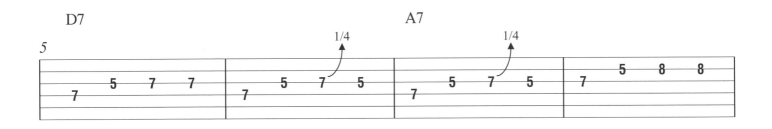

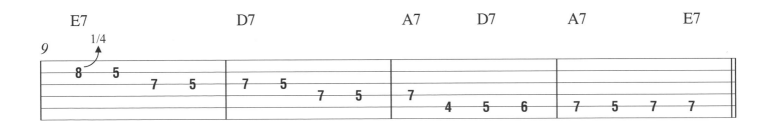

SOLO #11 – KEY OF A 🔊

#11 has a new bend to learn and also includes some new rhythms. The bends in all the measures except 4 and 7 are done with the third finger. The bends in bars 4 and 7 are done by pulling down a slight amount with the first finger. This may feel more difficult at first to move the string at all, but practice will make it easier than it seems.

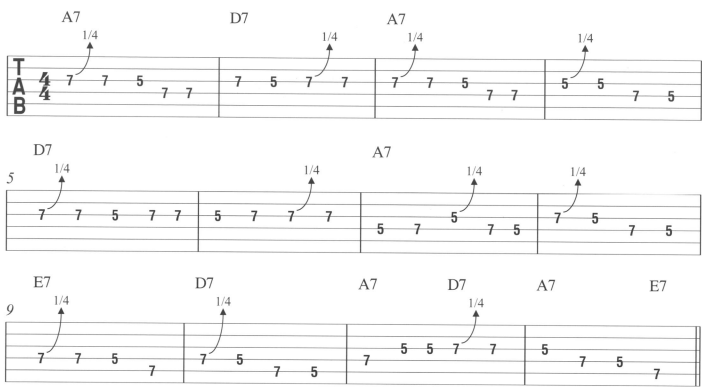

SOLO #12 – KEY OF A 🔊

The last solo is played more on the top strings than the others, a common choice in blues guitar solo-ing. All of the bends can be made with the third finger except in bars 3 and 12, in which the first finger should pull down on the string. In bar 12, barre the two notes on strings 2 and 1 with the first finger.

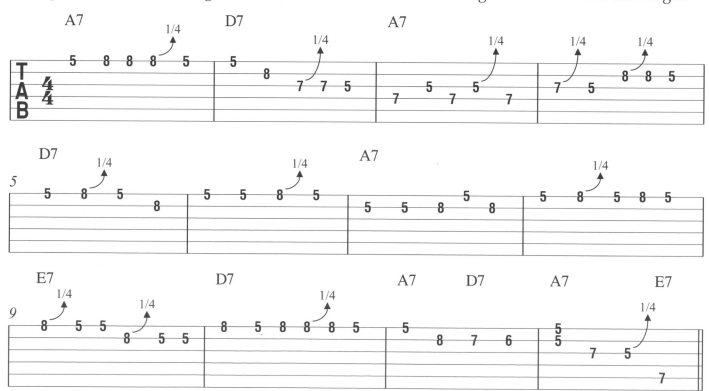